**FRIENDS
OF ACPL**

D1237678

AN OUTDOOR SCIENCE BOOK

PUDDLES
••• AND •••
PONDS

ROSE WYLER
PICTURES BY STEVEN JAMES PETRUCCIO

JULIAN ⓜ MESSNER

JULIAN MESSNER and colophon are
trademarks of Simon & Schuster, Inc.
Design by Malle N. Whitaker.
Manufactured in the United States of
America.

(Lib. ed.) 10 9 8 7 6 5 4 3 2 1

(Pbk.)   10 9 8 7 6 5 4 3 2 1

Library of Congress Cataloging-in-
Publication Data
Wyler, Rose.
Puddles and ponds / Rose
Wyler : pictures by Steven James
Petruccio.
   p.   cm.—(An outdoor science book)
Summary: Describes in simple text
and illustrations the plants and
animals that live in and around
ponds and other small bodies of
water. Includes instructions for
simple experiments.
1. Pond ecology—Juvenile
literature.   [1. Pond ecology. 2.
Ecology.]   I. Petruccio, Steven,
ill.   II. Title.   III. Series: Wyler, Rose.
Outdoor science book.
QH541.5.P63W95   1990   89-27588
574.5′26322—dc20   CIP
ISBN 0-671-66348-8   AC
ISBN 0-671-66352-6 (pbk.)

The author and publisher thank
Gary Hevel of the Smithsonian
Institution for his helpful suggestions.

Sloshing Around Mud Puddles

Rain, rain, and puddles fill up again.
Birds come to them for baths,
splashing in the muddy water.
They drink the water, too.
So do other animals.
Go sloshing around puddles and look for them.
You will have many surprises.
By the way, are your boots handy?

Bird

Some animals leave telltale footprints.
Dog footprints are easy to spot, but you may be
puzzled by footprints that look like little hands.
The animal that makes them is the raccoon.
Maybe one came to the puddle to wash its food.

Raccoons live almost everywhere—even in cities.
Yet people rarely see them, for they hide by day.
They come out only at night.

If you look around puddles in the country,
you might find hoof prints of deer.
Deer drink from puddles when they can.
Will you see any deer? Probably not.
They usually see you first and run away.

To find animals that won't run from you,
go looking for puddles that are a few days old.
Take along a jar and a magnifying glass
and look in the water for tiny creatures.

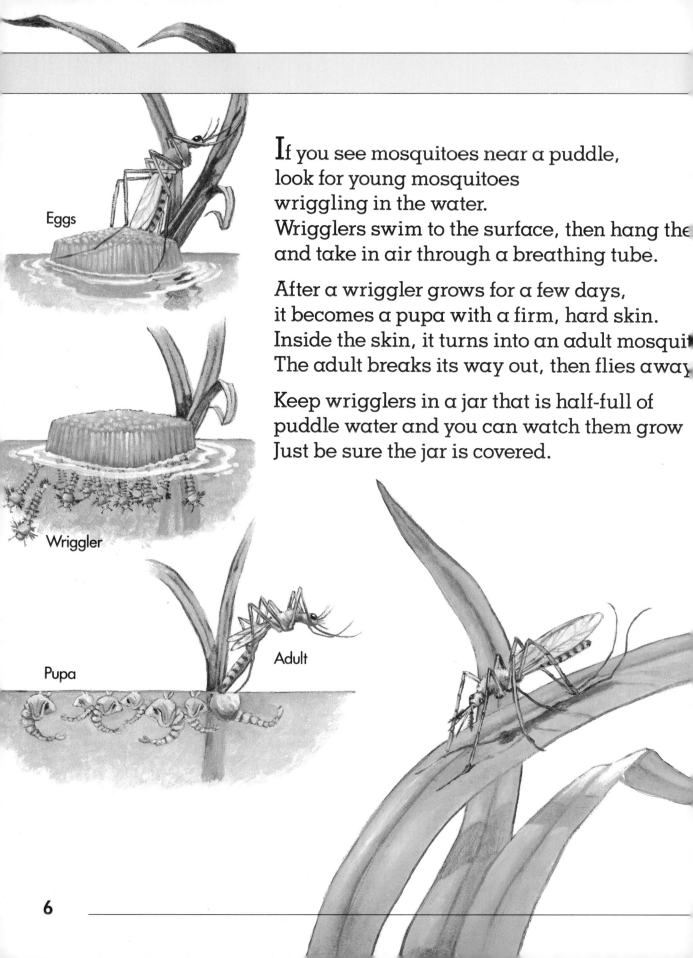

Eggs

Wriggler

Pupa

Adult

If you see mosquitoes near a puddle,
look for young mosquitoes
wriggling in the water.
Wrigglers swim to the surface, then hang the
and take in air through a breathing tube.

After a wriggler grows for a few days,
it becomes a pupa with a firm, hard skin.
Inside the skin, it turns into an adult mosqui
The adult breaks its way out, then flies away

Keep wrigglers in a jar that is half-full of
puddle water and you can watch them grow
Just be sure the jar is covered.

Mosquitoes are pests but they can be controlled.
One way to do this is to spray puddles with oil.
Oil clogs the breathing tubes of wrigglers
and kills them.

◆ ◆ ◆ ◆

Try this. Put a few drops of cooking oil on water in a jar with wrigglers in it and see what happens to them.

What food do wrigglers find in puddles?
Scoop up a jar of water from an old puddle.
Let the mud settle, then put a few drops
of the water on the inside of a jar lid.
Using your magnifying glass, look for specks
that are moving and for specks that are green
The ones that move are tiny animals;
the green ones are tiny plants.
Wrigglers eat them both.

As you check different puddles,
look for green scum growing in them.
The scum seems to be a gooey mess until
you examine it with a magnifying glass.
Then you see that this plant is made of threads
with green spirals running through them.
Some people think scum is ugly, but it is a sign
the water was not polluted by acid rain.
Acids make water sour and kill living things.

Volvox plant

Most old puddles teem with tiny living things
but you need a microscope to see them.
Is there a microscope that you can use?
If not, you can make one with a grownup's help.

Cut a metal strip from a can. Punch a hole in the center with a nail. Next, bend the strip at each end. Rest it on a pane of glass that is set across two piles of books. Prop a mirror underneath and tilt it to reflect light up through the glass. And now you have a microscope.

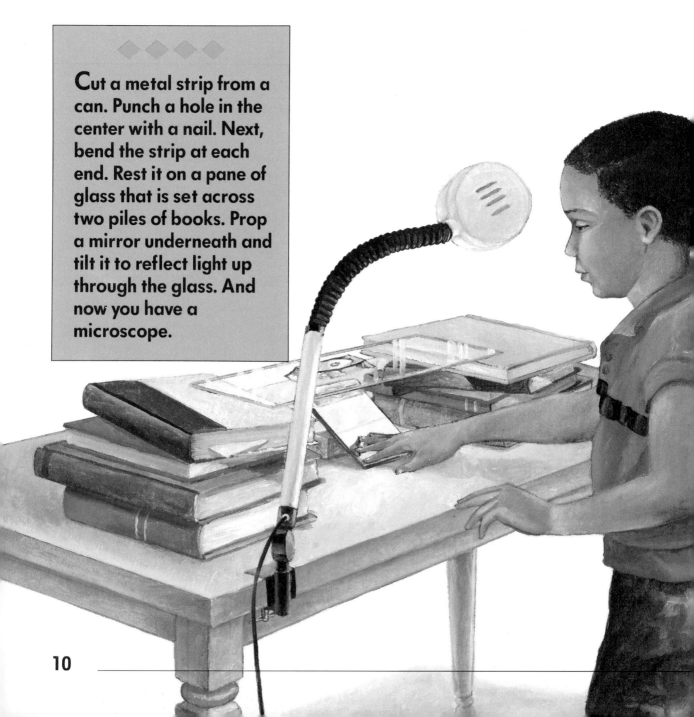

Using an eyedropper, put a drop of water from
an old puddle on the microscope glass.
Put the strip over it and fill the hole with
a drop of tap water to make a lens.
To focus it, press down on the strip.
You probably will see slipper animals swim,
water fleas hop, and wheel animals
creep on scum.
You might see other tiny creatures, too.

Of course, your homemade microscope
is not as good as a regular microscope.
Yet when you use it, a drop of puddle water
becomes a world of wonder.

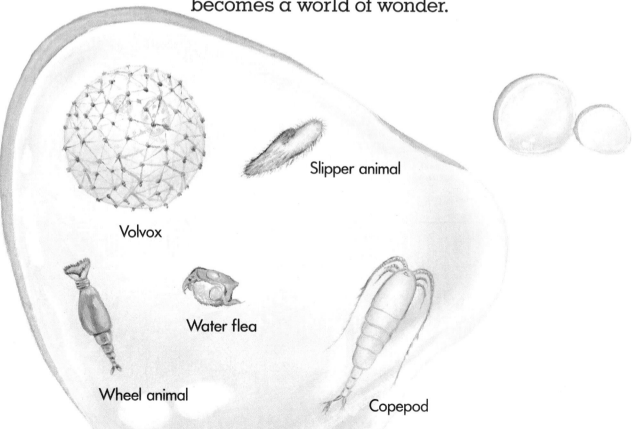

Slipper animal

Volvox

Water flea

Wheel animal

Copepod

Exploring a Pond

While puddles come and go, ponds rarely dry up.
They are deeper than puddles,
but not as deep as lakes.
In a pond the water is so shallow that
water lilies can take root along the bottom.
Plants usually grow all over a pond,
making it a water garden.

The plants provide food for many wild animals
and give them places to hide.
Getting near these animals isn't easy, but
that only adds to the fun of exploring a pond.

Before starting out, you will want to pack a kit with a strainer, a magnifying glass, some jars with lids, plastic cartons, and a water scope to use as you look down into the water.

◆ ◆ ◆ ◆

To make a water scope, cut a big hole in the bottom of a plastic carton. Cover the top with clear plastic wrap and hold it in place with a rubber band. You lower this end into the water and look through the other end.

When you go exploring, use your water scope
to look for snails.
You will find them creeping on pond plants.
Put some of the plants in a jar of water and
look along the stems for little globs of jelly.
The globs are snail eggs.
Perhaps you can see tiny snails in them.
You may even see some of them hatch.

Young snails

Snail

Snail eggs

Snails keep laying eggs all spring and summer.
But frogs lay eggs only in early spring.
You find them close to the shore in big clumps
with thousands of eggs in them.
Each egg is coated with jelly.
At first the eggs are round and black.
Then they change in shape and look like commas.
The commas twitch—they are tiny tadpoles.
Within ten days, they will wiggle out of the jelly.

Frog eggs

Use a strainer to scoop up some frog's eggs. Put them in a big jar with pond water and cover the jar. Then take it home and watch the eggs develop.

Tadpoles

It takes two to three months for a tadpole to become a frog.
Hind legs grow first, then front legs.
As the tail gets shorter, the tadpole stops breathing under water like a fish.
It starts breathing air, like a land animal, and soon becomes a grown-up frog.

Catch a frog, if you can, and watch it breathe. Its throat goes up and down while it takes in air through its nose.

You know fish are in a pond if you see a heron
looking into the water.
The bird is waiting for a fish that
it can grab with its sharp bill.

Another sign of fish are ripples in the water.
A fish makes them as it chases insects.
The fish could be a shiner or a sunfish.
Both are common in ponds that are not pollute

ou can bait little fish with crumbs, then
oop them into a jar and watch them swim.
t try to get near a painted turtle on a log!
e turtle will plop into the water and
ry under for a long time—perhaps for hours.
u might be able to catch one with a strainer
d to a long stick, or with a fish net.
you do, notice its webbed feet.
ose feet are a great help in swimming.

Dragonflies can look scary, but
these swift fliers do not bite or sting.
The young live in water and cannot fly.
You can find them if you float some pond pla
in a plastic carton.

While growing, the young dragonfly molts.
After each molt its wings are bigger.
Finally, it comes out of water to shed its skin
for the last time, and away it flies.

Adult Dragonfly

Young Dragonfly

Young Dragonfly

Watch water striders skim over the water and you wonder why they do not sink.
The water surface acts as a firm film and holds up the striders.
Their legs dent the film but do not break it.

Can you find any backswimmers?
They hang from the surface, taking in air, then they dive and swim underwater on their backs.
Follow one with a water scope, if you can.
But don't try to catch a backswimmer—it bites.

Water strider

Backswimmer

You can get dizzy watching whirligig beetle
They go round and round, hunting for food,
using two sets of eyes—one set that sees
above the water and one set that sees below

Get one into a jar of water and watch it swim
Listen to the beetle, too. It squeaks
as it rubs its wing covers against its body.
If it lifts those covers, it will start flying.
Then goodbye, whirligig.

Whirligig Beetle

Bring Them Back Alive

What will you do with your finds?
If it is allowed, take some home for an aquarium or small pool and put the rest back in the pond.

You can pack small plants and animals in jars and cartons of water with tight-fitting lids.
For a frog, use a big carton with a lid and just a little water.
A turtle can go in with it.
Bring back some extra pond water, too.

When you get home, examine the pond water
with a magnifying glass or a microscope.
If the water is not polluted, it looks alive.
Every drop teems with tiny plants and animals,
like the ones found in puddles.
Many of your finds eat these creatures,
so it's important to use some pond water
when you set up a new home for them.

Perhaps you and your friends can dig a hole for a mini-pond in a yard or on school grounds. You will need permission, of course.

◆ ◆ ◆ ◆

Use heavy plastic to line the hole. Cover it with soil, then with clean sand. Partly fill the hole with tap water. After a day, add the plants and animals and pond water.

If you want some water lilies, make a special trip for them and plant them immediately.

Lilies will attract insects and fish will eat them.
Turtles and frogs will eat them, too.
If a frog wanders away, it usually comes back.
In fact, a new frog might come with it.
A raccoon might come, too.

In very cold weather, ice will form in the pond.
If left outdoors, some creatures will die.
To prevent this, bring them indoors and
keep them in an aquarium.

Any jar, bowl, or tank with sides of clear glass
or plastic can be used for an aquarium.
Any size will do, but if you plan to keep lots
of pond animals, you will need a big tank.
Both pond and tap water can be used in it.

◆◆◆◆

To start an aquarium, cover the bottom with clean sand. Stick some pond plants in it. Then pour in water almost to the top. When it clears, add the animals.

If you have a frog or turtle, set up a rock or
stick that it can use when it is not swimming.
Remember, it breathes air.
A snail does, too, and will climb
above the water line of the tank to get air.

Do you have fish in the aquarium?
When fish breathe, they gulp down water.
They take oxygen gas from it with their gills,
then get rid of the water through gill slits.
Gulp, gulp—the fish are doing fine.

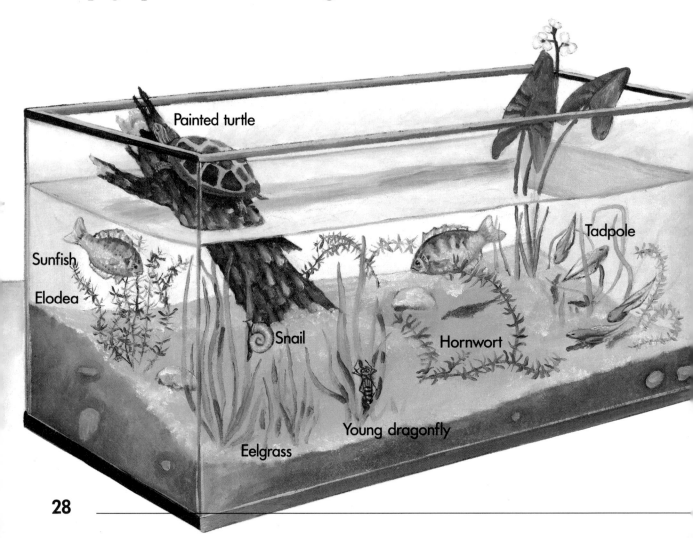

Painted turtle

Sunfish

Elodea

Snail

Eelgrass

Young dragonfly

Hornwort

Tadpole

Try this. Add a few drops of food coloring to a small glass of water. Fill an eyedropper with it. Next, put a fish in a white dish full of tap water. Bring the eyedropper close to its mouth and squeeze out a few drops. Then watch the colored water come out through the fish's gill slits.

Try this with a tadpole, too, and see how it breathes.

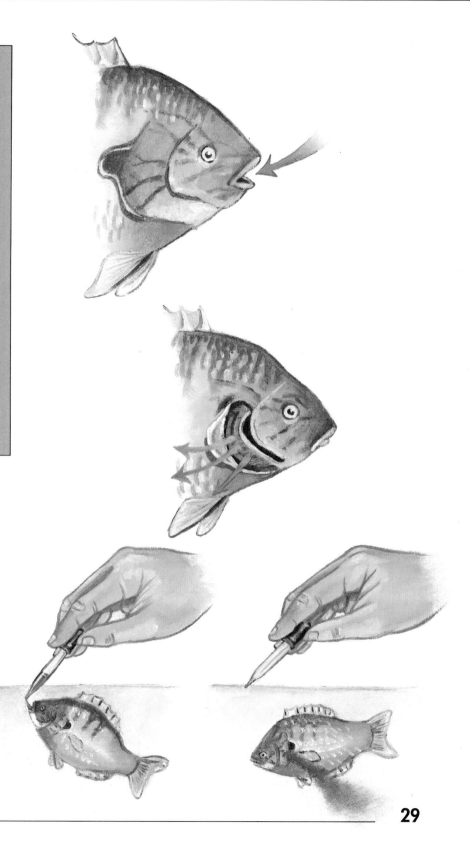

If you have plenty of plants in the aquarium,
the animals will have plenty of oxygen.
When bubbles form on pond weeds,
they are breathing out this gas.
Green scum and tiny plants breathe it out, too.
These plants also take in the gas that animals
breathe out, and that keeps the water fresh.

The plants will grow fast and provide food for
snails and some insects, small tadpoles, and fish.

Outdoors, the big fish and big tadpoles,
the frogs and turtles, eat smaller animals.
But you can keep them from doing this.

◆ ◆ ◆ ◆

Once a week drop some fish food from a pet store in the tank. Fish and tadpoles will gobble it up. To feed a frog or turtle, hook a small bit of meat on a paper clip, tie the clip to a string, and dangle it. A fish might go for this bait, too.

Except for the food that you add,
plants and animals live together in an aquarium
as they do outdoors.
By keeping them indoors, you can watch them
breathe, eat, and swim; and you can go on
exploring pond life all through the year.